SCUFFED-UP SHOES

JOHN M. TRAVIS

FOREWORD BY JOSEPH GOLDSTEIN & GIL FRONSDAL

EDITED BY COY F. CROSS II, PH.D.

Koho Pono, LLC

SCUFFED-UP SHOES
PUBLISHED BY KOHO PONO, LLC
CLACKAMAS, OREGON USA; HTTPS://KOHOPONO.COM

FIRST HARDCOVER EDITION 14APRIL2020

ISBN: 978-1-938282-30-0 (HARDCOVER)
ISBN: 978-1-938282-31-7 (PAPERBACK)
ISBN: 978-1-938282-32-4 (EBOOK)

FOREWORD BY JOSEPH GOLDSTEIN & GIL FRONSDAL
EDITED BY COY F. CROSS II, PH.D

Scuffed-up shoes

Longing for ground,
Scuffed-up shoes,
A flower opens.

Dedication

This book is dedicated to the students of the Dharma, who have been supported by Spirit Rock and Mountain Stream as venues for these teachings.

TABLE OF CONTENTS

FOREWORD
by Joseph Goldstein

The depth and breadth of John Travis' poetry reflect his own extraordinary life. We first met in the late 60's when he had been traveling around the ashrams and mountains of India. His inner compass was always aligned with the true north of wisdom and compassion, seeking them out wherever they were to be found. And in this volume of poetry, he shares his great, open, wise heart with us all.

Author of <u>Mindfulness: A Practical Guide to Awakening</u>

FOREWORD
by Gil Fronsdal

"The heart knowing its way,
Stepping on the old path"
John Travis

These poems give you, the reader, a direct view into John's heart. At the same time, they turn you back onto yourself to give a clearer view of your own heart, including the good, the bad, and the liberating. These poems are just as much an intimate expression of John's embracing all his humanity as they are an encouragement for you to do the same. In this book, John reveals his lows and highs, challenges and joys, pain and freedom. Inspiringly, he also describes the journey from one to the other, from darkness to light, from suffering to the end of suffering.

Many of these poems were written for Dharma talks John gave on meditation retreats he was teaching. But John never just teaches, he is always practicing with whatever his life brings. These poems are, therefore, not just teachings to benefit the retreat participants, they are how John gives voice to his spiritual journey. This can include the journey during one session of meditation, over the course of the retreat, or spanning years and decades. Through the poems, we can witness John's strong instinct to dive into his inner pain and then find a way out into a vast sense of peace and freedom.

His journeys are journeys of mindfulness that unfold by staying present for whatever is happening. The poems are a testament to the power of settling into one's present moment experience. Returning to the breath, sitting in the fire, and staying still in the midst of life are the ingredients John uses for his mindfulness journey. Because many of the poems end with experiences of freedom, clarity, and peace, they are a tribute to the effectiveness of Dharma practice.

Delightful lines that represent the journey to liberation are,

> *"Climbing slowly out of the fog of delight,"*

followed later in the poem by,

> *"Freeing oneself from the fog,*
> *the moon shines on the great mountain."*

Many of the poems contain "turning phrases", which can change your mind with sudden unexpected perspectives. If you allow yourself to be both pulled into the poems and receptive to being changed, these turning phrases can stop the mind, expand the mind, and even liberate the mind. For example, what happens to you if you imagine,

> *"A picture frame bigger than the cosmos"?*

And what is evoked by reading,

> *"We were never not whole"?*

This is followed a few lines later with,

> *"We have to give up everything to sit here."*

Some turning phrases may turn you around to take a deeper look at yourself. For example, what might you understand about yourself when reading the following poem?

> *"Before freedom speaks*
> *you must know,*
> *know you lost something"*

And what areas of your life does the following phrase describe?

> *"What seemed like a battle becomes a symphony."*

How do you reflect on yourself when reading

"This inner-tube of self
Slowly losing air?"

As a co-teacher of retreats, I sat next to John many times as he began and ended his Dharma talk with a poem composed that afternoon. It was quite moving to hear him read the poem because his voice carried the range of emotions the words represented. At the start of his reading, there was usually a sense of raw honesty, vulnerability, and personal struggle. By the end of the reading, his voice carried his deep faith, love, and certainty for the depths and fullness of spiritual realization. One delightful expression of this realization that expands it beyond the domain of personal attainment is,

"You were always whole.
The mountain was you."

In between the start and finish of his talks, many of the poems expressed the commitment to practice with whatever struggles one has. This commitment would be expressed in many ways. In one poem in this book, it is with the instruction,

"Remembering to invite that part that limps"

In another, it is through searching for the answer to the following question,

"How can the fury and the silence coexist?"

But it was not only the words of the poems that John read that had a big impact on the retreat participants. Often, the biggest impact was the transmission of the depth of practice. Clearly, John was tapping into all he had realized in the course of his years of practice and in the fullness of his awakening. John would become part John who had lived with great struggles, part wise elder, part shaman, and part conduit for the truth. In doing this, his poems became transmissions by which meditation practitioners, in their receptive state, could begin to recognize the truth in themselves. And if not the truth, they might have a felt sense of the sincerity with which to plunge into the Dharma.

John's poems are gifts. I am grateful for hearing many of them and now I am grateful to have them in this book. As I finish this foreword, I end with two of John's lines from poems in this book. They are words that can represent what John conveys to all of us:

"The heart shines forever"

and

"Leaving only gratitude".

- Gil Fronsdal

THE TREK

Two Views

Looking down again at the dusty road.
Why is it
when one longs for home,
the backpack and the seedy foreign rooms appear so
limited?
Yet at home, the closets, boxes, possessions
seem entangling.
Is it possible to look beyond this self-obsession?

A spinning dervish,
obsessed with tell-tale signs of thinking-planning,
Remembering
the place in the high mountains,
with the heart, unbounded and untroubled,
Where nobody knows who you are—or cares—not even
yourself.

True! A home waits.
Unfettered by possessive grasping,
allowing for the circling of wagons
to reflect community vision,
A small village temple,
intwined in the complexity of details,
calling again and again for simplicity,
pure heart—clear minds.

Actions chewed on—lasting for many generations.
Patiently waiting so the doors can stay open;
giving back
to the thousands of years
of awakening.
Knowing somehow this will go on and on,
beyond you—beyond me...

February 21, 2011

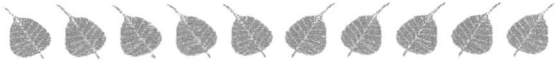

War Raging

Trembling inside my armor,
War raging,
Leaping off into the moat,
Landing softly on the breath.

2001

Rim of Time

Sitting on the rim of time
Waiting for the breath
Some foothold on the mountainside
Some place to take a stand

Over and over again... disappointed
Until that "that grasps"
Floats on the eddy of time,
Saying,
     "This is body found,
      A river carrying everything
      And nothing."

February 19, 2005

Bodh Gaya

Mind like alligator
Touches chest
Opening big jaws
But only to snap on empty space.
Few if any stories
The jaws snapping to no end
Yet in moments between breaths
A memory of one moment in Bodh Gaya
Which illuminated Gautama 2,500 years ago
And for this one, a moment,

Pointing in that direction just 36 years ago
One finished to full Buddhahood
The other began a lifetime of practicing and deepening.

Retreat Bodh Gaya; January 24, 2006

The Scent of Freedom

One turns away from this cycle of becoming
—Shaken by the force of habit and longing—
Knowingly dragging the bones of the 10,000 sufferings.

Why is it that when you get it
The grasping, clinging, attachment seems so apparent?

Dragon spewing rocks and fire,
beginning this courageous battle of unburdening the "self",
Heroes, generously giving themselves to a journey plagued by doubt—knowing—
they had to mix the fear with the faith.
Blind once more, resting in the faith of the Pilgrim who broke free 25 centuries ago,
Befriending the sworn enemy of clarity and heart,
No possibility of turning around when the scent of freedom
—Registering the truth of such a fleeting world—
is close at hand.

One sits so quietly listening to the flow of sensations and thoughts,
No longer disturbed by doubts or the need to know,
Everything is like water flowing through one's palms and fingers.

This deep sense that one has left behind the ferocity of a painful world,

This immunity of the great silence, giving birth to confidence and delight,

One has made it past the dark shores and the burning buildings

To a place on that first hill, seeing the fog in the distance and the body of the great mountain.

This simple longing to reach the thin and glorified heights of a promised freedom

One gently descends into this foggy valley consumed by its beauty.

Trees with delicate moss,

Perfect flowers with enchanted bees,

Streams with perfect clarity, nothing out of place,

Recognizing growing joy, tranquility and happiness,

Completely enthralled by the lightness of being and virtues of concentration,

Suddenly recognizing that one still had a ways to go before reaching the great mountain.

Oh my!

Shades of impermanence, twinges of suffering and personality still linger.

Climbing slowly out of the fog of delight,

Coming to a vista,

Sinking deeply into the knowledge and body of truth,

Kneeling down to drink the tears of last year's realizations.

Looking up from this pristine hill, the great mountain is that much closer.

A steep path leads down through rocks and bramble bushes.

Stumbling down through heavy fog temporarily hides the great mountain.

The clear austerity and strength of one who knows, "There is no turning around."

One weaves one's way down, down to the bottom of the ravine,

Disenchanted by the sense doors or even the conjured stories and beliefs,

Everything steady, a deep equanimity, allows one to climb up through the steepness.

Leaving behind the sleeping world, non-attached in dispassionate steps, one climbs.

Freeing oneself from the fog, the moon shines on the great mountain,

Lighting up all the corners of one's own mind and heart.

Now your bag is empty, no need for words or even inspiration.

Arriving at the gateless gate

March 23, 2013

Listening

Who knew I lived here
Perched on this dying branch,
Shivering inside this heated dome,
Allowing the stars to shine?

River Rushes—Buddha Floats

Sitting hour after hour,
No end in sight.

Time rushes downstream,
Holding on for dear life.

Inner-tube of self,
Slowly losing air.

Current pulling one out into the unknown

Struggling for shore once again,
One lets go
    Of inner tube
    No struggle
In pure amazement floating
    "Look, Mom, no hands,
    No feet,
    No body,
    Oops, no me."

When clarity comes finally,
The Buddha crashes
    On his bottom
    Cracking the center
    Revealing golden light.

January 4, 2005

The Split

Skin and bone, muscle and blood,
You, who in your youth I betrayed,
Abandoning you for my stories, ideas, dreams,
Leaving you in some dumpster in the Haight Ashbury,
Hoping no one would notice.
But you, like a sly fox,
shadowed me to India,
barefooted, hair matted and greasy,
bowels bubbling and gurgling,
Waiting again and again to be noticed.

Finally sitting down,
You right next to me, shyly,
Mirroring my every move
First you scold me,
tearing at my knees, crushing my back,
bringing me down so my face is on your floor.
Me, wanting so bad to dig you out of my cells,
and throw you away.
You, claiming your rightful home,
washed in tears; we walk hand in hand towards the cliff.

Spring 1999

River

Hands and feet are desperate for solid ground
    Caught in the current
Mind racing for a sandbar
Heart in an eddy turning and turning
    Small voice
    Interior angel
    Buddha's practice
"Let go, let go, let go!"

Silence... struggling stops...
One moment of pure attention
A thousand eons fade
The heart shines forever.

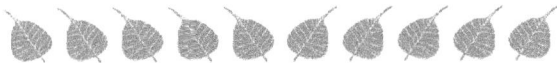

Sitting on the Edge of the World

Dropping in—smack into the middle of your world
Silence crackling through my bloodstream
Oh, I can guess
You came to set something free
But once again
    nothing
    but
    change

New teachers, new faces
The boat you so carefully steadied rocked
Knowing this feeling of empty seats with familiar socks
and shawls

Vanishing into the rain and fog
You know
    the one who pretended
    to have it all
    together
Feeling again the loneliness of those who bowed and
walked away

Openly aware of those still here, all who hold you now
How still can I be in this stilled world?
How still can I be in this still world?

Is it holding the old stories?
Or being battered and beaten?
Is it the lightness of being, which radiates in the 10,000
directions?

We who have arrived can only bow to your truth
But the height of the mountain calls us all—
    stretches out
    before us
    as our common
    destination

March 16, 2012

The Tattered Self

Sometimes walking along the path
the traveler encounters his own needy shadow.
Perplexed by the question,
"That can't be me?"
The mirror must be confused.
It's just a visitation from a ghost, some proximity of the
real me.
Deep down, knowing that the confrontation
was again pulling one towards one's own beckoning
where the revelation of the path through the mountains
could be a way to silence the one in the mirror.

Oh my! How many "me's" have I created?
Every fear and hope creating a newer version.

Finally having to stop.
Not turning around or looking ahead,
but standing—face in hands—
shedding tears for all the lost selves
Meticulously crafted so I wouldn't have to know
it would end as a dead end, everything redistributed.

Speaking in a low voice, hoping the other parts won't
hear,
This hidden silence, slowly deconstructing

the tortured and unassuming faces, or should I say
"masks".

A moment again where the mountain path is
so obscured by the many stories
painted so colorfully across masks,
distorting both eyes and ears,
comes back into focus.

Winding its way towards the heavens,
revealing snow and wind, to a high and rocky loneliness,
A place where we can take back
the image and break the mirror of "this and that".
At last, letting the body carry this heart and mind,
Slowly letting the self recede in the amazement,
Being blessed by the relative and absolute.

February 1, 2013

Two Legs
(wings of awakening)

Now having found the mountain
Looking up, covered in mist.
Heart sinks.
Inner teacher says,
"Stop! Feel your feet!
Look only at your next step!"
Two legs,
Pointed up the Mountain.
Listening to the many voices,
Waiting for that one word
 that points the compass to that original face,
Pinnacle within your own mind,
This leg of wisdom.

That other leg,
 stiff, held by the old pains, memories, protections,
Only moved when the heart softens,
Giving it that gentle touch,
"I have been with you, all of these years.
We will climb together.
Knowing all those that we have touched
Climb with us."

Dalai Lama's refrain calls us over and over again,
"Don't give up!"

March 30, 2005

walking for Days

Day by day, stripping our known world,
ups seem endless, downs not so different,
finally reaching a temple,
ancient power and heart,
someplace where magic and the ordinary
rest within the dark and the light.

Given the deep privilege to speak,
"What you see has no core or substance,
yet truly is exactly as it seems."
We wrestle with this paradox,
giving the self a twirl.

Trek through Upper Mustang, Nepal; June 1, 2014

The Crashing Waves

Day and night relentless fury
Waves pound out every thought
Waves pound out every emotion

Sometimes believing one is stranded on the edge of
The edge of time
There is silence between the waves

How can the fury and this silence coexist?

Drifting sometimes towards a past,
Where magic and bitters fall short
Of anything
As real as
The sea mimicking the breath...
Or is it
The breath that mimics the sea?

Feeling old tugs,
The mind tracks itself,
Looking for its own source,
Bedazzled by its own constructions.
Gently giving over
To the waves

A mind twisting to find meaning
Turns itself
Inside out
Only to find this body
sensing itself

Oh yes! It was all about surrender.

The mind was at home to begin with.
Being lived through a body
A heart washed in gratitude.
Rising, falling, rising, falling...

February 15, 2013

Healing

Waiting patiently for something,
Someone to appear,
Graciously sitting,
Deflecting stories,
Breath breathing itself,
Slowly, painfully, taking off your mask,
Only to grow another,
Building it back one imagining at a time,
Cheeks, nose, mouth, ears
With that little, little thought
Of grandeur or impoverishment.

Oh! Brother/Sister
How to heal that which is whole?
You think, out-think, out-maneuver.
Or possibly swallow all the light.

Ah! But Buddha pointed
Couldn't we skip this part,
The light inside the dark?

Sitting

I went for a blessing today, was given a holy pouch,
spiriting it off to the desert, lo and behold bursting open,
a great bonfire,
first revealing a filthy, tattered, crumpled cloth stamped in large letters
RESISTANCE,
And another spotted with dried blood, snot, phlegm, bile, written in calligraphy
IMPATIENCE
the third a crisp white starched envelope embossed with gold letters
BOREDOM
Putting them on the altar,
They smoldered without burning,
Lighting up the hut keeping the cold out.
We sat together
Foe, teacher, friend.

Clear Path

Knowing this is a desperate journey,
Untangling our projections and stories,
Sitting on the edge of our history,
Knowing that refusing entry would only
Pull us farther and farther out to sea.
Resolving not to leave this fire for another day,
But to sit in the center attending to breath after breath,
With this simple refrain, "I am here. I am here."

Aware, deep down, knowing breath could be shallow or
deep, sometimes long or short,
Always attempting to catch it.
Releasing, softening, breathing,
Supported by this eternal presence,
Life breathing itself.

How great to know it has worked for eons.
Slowly dissolving the old darkness;
Tentacles from the past dissolving.
The power of the breath releasing multiple contractions,
Giving way to the certainty,
"This breath is enough."

Awakening assured by our lineage,
So clearly spelled out.

March 7, 2015

🍃🍃🍃🍃🍃🍃🍃🍃🍃

The Time When Nothing Works

Honorable Seeker. Pilgrim,
Wonder if everyone was wrong?
This sitting by the bank of this heart stream,
Listening, listening to this endless chatter,
Playing old movies, dramas, stories,
Endlessly writing new scripts from the
Tasks of our life.
Sometimes brilliant, other times dropping
Off to sleep trance dance land,
Head bobbing.
It tastes so good,
That sweet sensual delight
Captured forever and not at all.
Tell me again why sit here
Body fidgeting, screaming to be somewhere else,
Anywhere else.

🍃🍃🍃🍃🍃🍃🍃🍃🍃

Reflection

Looking into a deep pool,
Staring at the reflection,
Face all drawn up in seriousness,
Saying loudly, "Is this one me?"
Vomiting,
Mask begins to peel off,
Layer by layer.

Teacher, "Is reflection real?"
Looking down into pool,
Somewhere between the grasses
The last layer of mask fades

Leaving the heart known by itself.
Pool has no bottom
Nothing to put back on
Intrinsically silent.

The great sigh of ease.

A Better Me

I went looking for a better me today,
One that sparkled in the sun.
Inviting Resistance and Impatience to accompany me.
We again took the wrong fork in the road.
Bowing deeply, I went my own way
Leaving all
    the many voices
        behind.

The bushes, inflamed by the spring sun,
Gave completely to the bees.
I knew right then,
"Surrender to the bee taking whatever it wants."
Nectar
    moved by
        invisible wings.

Called my friends Resistance and Impatience back.
Held myself, we were all together again.
But nobody spoke this time.
The sky
    held us
        without questions.

March 15, 2005

Bodyness

The wind whistling through this valley
Maybe it could blow the many thoughts,
Stories and feelings out through the hills,
Scattering them for miles and miles.

Yet today setting on this sore bum,
Knees a little creaky,
Not sure why I would want to inhabit
This ignored body.

Difficulty pulling buoyant mind down,
Down into this skittish body,
Staying only a moment then off again,
Prancing around, hoping to think myself,
Out of all these discomforts.

Yet remembering this sacred and enchanted place,
Asking only to surrender to a body,
Steeped in its own natural liveliness,
Body inhabiting body.

Awareness has this home,
Destined to feel itself one breath at a time,
Making nothing out of all of this.
Resting in its totality.

Body in body.
Heart full.

May 6, 2013

Purification

Deep below the ledge
Another mask is revealed.
Is that you, original face?
Heart leaping?
But who is that child in the corner,
Eyes sparkling, who knows love so well?

January 1, 2003

Vajrapanni (Skillful Means)

Sitting in the center of the circle,
Luminous perfection,
The mirror unstained,

Heating up, hotter and hotter,
Melting that frozen moment held in the closet of
memory,
Die, just die!
Blue jays, like great cheerleaders stirring you on,
Die, die!
The past holds no future here.
The whirling fans hum the eternal mantra
"Letting go... letting go."

Like a prizefighter
Wanting that last win,
Staggering from hits
And bruises of the old scars,
Bandaged so many times before,
Same old stories
Told over and over,
Hoping that somehow
The ending will be different.

Sitting in the center of the circle,
The breath reappears.
Demons came to visit today
Asking for my support,
So I gave it to them,
But tomorrow maybe not.

With friends like these
Who says the armoring
Of the heart won't melt?

Lotus Eaters

Dropping thoughts like Lotus petals
On this ground
Like a fierce dragon shooting flames
In all directions
Settling back, hands open

November 23, 2002

Clarity

Sitting on this staircase of time,
This narrow staircase,
A hollow thought captures me,
Pulling me back to the bluest moments
Where silence is forgotten,
The faces of love lost,
Trolls through the waters of memory
Looking for a place where freedom could never exist.
Grabbing a thought,
Letting it roar through my best intentions
Like a wild fire on a windy day,
Knowing somehow nothing ever really goes away
Until it has taught us what we need to know.
Finally, releasing it back into nowhere,
Tired of all these endless thoughts.

Awareness Takes Care of Itself

The mind, like a great tiger,
Waits for a thought to pounce on,
Once identified, it makes its move;
Making it more real than the world around it,
Creating worlds of succulent identification.

Today, from one thought,
I created Buddha realms.
Layer upon layer,
Like a swollen boil,
It popped.

At first, stranded in the present,
Only to awaken to the peace
And contentment of the simple,
Ordinary awareness that holds
The Buddha fields of right here.
Leaning back; not disturbed by anything,
All experience empty.
Need for "for or against" nowhere to be found.
Thoughts float by like clouds
Letting everything pass by.
No place to stand,
Awareness takes care of itself.

Root Institute, Bodh Gaya; India; February 11, 2006;
Full Moon

The Medicine Pouch

Hesitantly, standing between worlds.
The gate is open, dear heart.
What kind of medicine are you carrying in your pouch,
Pilgrim?
Turkey feathers, lizards' tails, a worm's body,
A small brush of deer hair,
A ray from the full moon,
A tattered picture of Shangri-La?

Is it enough, these few things,
To stand by the high tide
Without being swept by the tsunami of your life?

Buddha whispered from that deep place within,
"Medicine pouch full.
You're enough.
These few things enough,"
Opening your whole body-heart to the deep water
Pulling you out into the world

Everything held in the original ordinariness,
A picture frame bigger than the cosmos.

March 24, 2005

Compassion

Breathing, in-out, heavy pain, fear,
Planning, breath, in-out, hearing, burning.
Enough already!

Thinking, thinking, thinking,
Like a gazelle bounding across the plains,
"Give me the answer!
Wrap it up in a nice package.
Can't we go home now?"

Community melted down by afternoon heat,
Little flies awakening the hearing.
"Where is this all going?"

Searching everywhere inside.
Small flutter.
Laying the body on the altar.
Like the smallest crack in time.
Golden glow.
Having searched the universe,
Mind resting in heart
"Oh! That's how it works!"

August 12, 2005

Caught Between Two Worlds

The marvels of the bougainvillea and the hibiscus,
Colors that hold one in softness and beauty.
Delighted by the visible world,
The sea in its blue and turquoise—so inviting.

Butterflies dancing in warm Thai breezes.
The jungle and perfect temperature of water and air.
With the outer world so enchanted,
Why see, feel the transparency of such an ideal world?

Easy to want to keep this physical world in such perfect
order.
Yet a mind trained to disassemble, deconstruct the
visible,
Releasing the entire known world into its truth of
Its dependent co-arising,
The sheer emptiness of it all turns one to the
unconstructed.

One could call this the invisible world
Someplace where consciousness releases the seen world,
Dancing on the edge of the known parameters of the
senses,
Resting between the edge of sea and land.

The marvels of living in a fleeting world,
Sometimes engrossed, absorbed in little moments of the senses,
Other times, feeling the sadness of your irreversible time.
The world, our bodies fading from youth, midlife, now old age.

Such a small crack, needing trained attention,
Releasing all fabrications, infinitesimal moment after infinitesimal moment,
Softening the heart so beauty and sadness hold together.
Truth giving answer
How can I help knowing all this?

February 18, 2013

Just Another Pilgrim

Looking out with longing eyes,
Recognizing that in youth there was some solace,
Adventuring always to another trail,
Leading you to some fork in the road,
The thrill of the new places never seen before.
Somewhere inside
Longing for a higher road
Destined like any traveler to be subject to the
unpredictable.

Yet, today, sitting quietly, realizing
Even the trials of midlife;
Tore at the soles of the old pilgrim's
Bruised and scarred feet,
Leaving his armor broken and bent,
Knowing the learning is all about the sunset now.

The bravado of yesterdays' sunrises touching deeply,
As the aware mind surrenders to its likes and dislikes,
Not buying anything anymore,
Just the senses and thoughts experiencing themselves.
Control was a fantasy, the freeing of which was
everything.

The wings, even broken in places,
Now knowing even the slightest breezes
Allow one to glide through a contracted world.
Freedom was in everything, sliding softly into ease,
The small tears of grace being so grateful for living.

All this just to find faith—even so very small.
Heart feeling its own wonder.
No longer needing the footpath of the Pilgrim
But the wonder of still being alive
Every place, giving everything.
Hallelujah.

February 13, 2013

Pilgrimage toward Awakening

So why would I want to climb this mountain?
Maybe it was yesterday, last week, last month, last
year, sometime long ago... long before now.

A lightning bolt cut through the darkness of mind's
eternal chatter
Revealing a majestic snow-covered peak.
For a minute* moment the clouds parted.
Somehow, not knowing if it was real or a dream,
Some impulse, deep down,
knows, "No time to waste."

The heart frozen
the mind enmeshed in fog
body not found

Knowing the harsh need to change us was at hand.
Sitting down in remedial silence
watching everything like the sages, seers, seekers,
listening, listening, breathing, fidgeting,
thoughts like streams of every color
darting off, landing nowhere.

---

* minute (my-NOOT)

Was it five days... nine days?
Waiting for that inner compass,
that trusted voiceless instinct,
like a sleepwalker
surrendering the mind to the heart.

Humbly walking without seeing,
zero visibility,
heart knowing its way,
nervously letting ourselves down
on this old path
trodden by so many courageous
seekers, wanderers, pilgrims.

Letting go of the ground we stand on,
nervously clinging to every day,
so for one moment
the breath, breathe all beings.
Yes! You were always whole.
The mountain was you.

March 4, 2010

Homecoming

As I was pushing on,
The Wall appeared.
Falling to my knees,
I cursed it.
One time
Closing down,
Silent,
Withdrawn,
Letting go of the longing (wanting) to arrive.
Out of some deep passage-way,
My hands begin to move across the cold smooth stones,
Fingers already knowing where to go.
Finally coming around the corner,
Opening not only the eyes but everything,
Slowly getting up walking on,
No questions, no hesitation,
Opened to a breath,
A step,
A breath,
A step,
A breath,
A step.

Kalachakra

Listening to the drone of the Dalai Lama,
Thousands of monks,
Perched above in the retreat hut...
The sounds
Stirring this heart
In this natural amphitheater.

There is a way of being still.
Silencing the sound outside and inside,
Knowing even the stones speak,
Robbing my words and thoughts,
While the great silence has stolen me.

July 1, 2014

Scuffed-Up Shoes

THE
CUSHION

First Day

Like a great blazing fire,
Body came to rest on the cushion—
Fired up to stay awake and present
Only to find bittersweet drifting off
Old stories held court
While body cried out,
"Pay attention to me, I'm the most important."
Everything demanded attention.
Nobody got first choice today.
Maybe enlightenment can wait.
"Where are my car keys?"

March 30, 2005

A New Life

A majestic Buddha sitting in the center of our hall,
Resting so silent in the midst of our world.
While we, on the other hand,
Squirm, fidget, imagining, "Everyone's still but me."

Chasing our smallest thoughts,
Quelling our gripped desire—over and over again
Living in a world; just missed—
Another mind wave drawing us out... again.

Somewhere in the Cloud
All our old lives are stored—images,
Plans, memories, dreams, thoughts, emotions—
Pulling us towards what end?

How to wake up in the midst of all this?
Make friends with all these complex monologues,
Could it be as simple as bowing to each new arrival—
Befriending even the difficult and frightened parts?

Firmly establishing yourself—
Once again finding no place better?
Than this flimsy breath,
A grounded body,
And a wayward mind—with everything settled.

The heart like a shy puppy
Begins to crawl out of its hiding place,
Excited to be in the wonder of a new life.

May 15, 2015

All Day Is Still All Day

There is this leaning forward,
    checking in,
    again and again.
Could we be near a new beginning
    or a dreaded end?
I was thinking…
    oops, that could be the problem.
Always this imagining; having learned how to keep it
simple.

Sitting on a bench
    near the hall;
    tree miraculously budding.
Loosening my grip
    on these sense doors
    and fickle thoughts.
Sitting in the tranquil presence
    of my own body.
Breath, breathing itself, remembering
    this leaning into time only a habit.

We sat together
    —Awareness and these sense doors—
    in this grand and marvelous world.
Studying this inner/outer landscape,
    hoping to find something.

But then there was just "phooey" and "wow"
    couldn't find a thing.
Some grand awakening will have to wait
    until next retreat. Phooey!

I knew this was all so very simple.
    Clear mind,
      seeing for miles and miles.
A mysterious heart
    holding everything
    in open spaciousness,
Anchoring awareness in the body
    knowing the ease
    as the destination.

So I practice not moving into tomorrows.
    No leaning into time,
    planning some pleasure or impossible escape.
But resting in the natural peace and ease.
    That is the natural peace and ease.
    Confident in how it goes.

May 23, 2012

The White Heron

The white heron,
standing so still,
dignity of posture,
like the yogis in our hall,
knowing somehow
to draw ourselves back,
back into a center of safety,
consumed solely by the center of our own flames.

Burning the old,
the old stories,
wishes, fears, and desires,
your own voice calling to yourself,
only heard by yourself,
back, back from the brink of the remembering
to this place where the white heron stands.
Breath, breathing you.

Untouched by a shredded past,
an incomprehensible future;
resting like the white heron.
Only the dignity of the posture remains
blessed by the faculties of our senses
knowing somehow there is no other world
than this, simply this.

There is this small point
—infinite point—
where the world divides.

One road leads back,
back into the flames of becoming
—voice speaks too quickly—
desperately searches through the crowded years
where life's hopes and fears
can be played
in this game of winning
—and probably losing—
grasping tightly, capturing, imprisoning,
keeping it for all time.

And then there's this other path, old path,
caught in the miracle of ordinariness,
bewilderment,
the price of sand slipping through our fingers,
knowing somehow that we have to surrender
leaving behind the hopes and fears in the grasping,
resting nowhere,
falling on your knees,
knowing somehow that the heart knows its way from
here... on.

Retreat at Spirit Rock Meditation Center; March 16, 2010

Endings

Did you say it was over?
You mean I'm kicked out,
Back to the world I so carefully crafted?

How could this be?
I just got here.
You must have a plan,
All this work
Just to get so sensitive.

It was raining and dark,
Both inside and outside,
When I arrived.
Sitting quietly,
Again and again,
And so,
The clouds on the inside
Began to thin,
Day by day.

You knew you came
To give up some of the old
And frightened parts.

Remembering some faith,
The Sun having been there all along,

Waiting,
Waiting patiently,
Day after day,
For you to breathe into your heart once again.
Standing firm,
Knowing for sure that the winds of change,
Demanding everything,
Only to pull you back into the complexity of your life.
Maybe this time,
Pausing a little longer,
Listening,
Listening to something below the chatter.
Heart little more at ease.
One sings one song.
Mercy. Mercy.

Retreat at Spirit Rock Meditation Center; March 19, 2010

The Small Crack

Before the flame ignites the world
Sitting close to the breath
A voice hesitant and trembling a little

"Is there a choice here or is it just habit?"
Bamboozled by a world turning too fast?

It's such a small movement
How life's marvels lead to this moment's hesitation.
How easily our wings could catch fire
Or help us soar above a meditation hall.

Oh yes! A small crack revealed, rising and floating
In the mist of my own mind.
Can't you tell the difference, sir, between
Being pulled into or being pushed away?

Oh my! This slight stumble, caught again,
Entranced by this cycle of becoming
Weeds float on the surface
Knowing somehow
The weeds keep reproducing themselves.

This is about insight.
Courageously studying the laws of grasping,
Befriending the truth of dependent origination,

54

Knowing some days I wish I didn't or couldn't know.

Yet readiness for quiet brings me down to my knees
A moment where I don't choose liking or disliking
But sit in the center of longing without movement.
The sky slowly begins to open.

Recognizing that resting in that crack between worlds
Brings the blessings of an adult mind
And the heart of the child held with ease
Freeing oneself
This bright mind
Illuminates this impermanent world.

March 14, 2013

Crow Speaks

In the sanctuary of this practice,
Held so keenly by the two-winged crow,
Bursting with its chatter,
Sending its message from retreatants to the heavens,
Perched on the pinnacle of our hall,
Viewing our own longing for freedom,
Covered over by the dark door of our own hope and fear,
We sat quietly, unruffled by the unseen.
The weight of our own shadows
Slowly dissolved under the intense light of our own awareness,
The great light of our own goodness shined from behind,
Believing that we would be blinded,
Slowly we turned away
Directly into the sun.
Words, ideas, and images dissolved in the light of this truth.
Finally exhausted, we stopped struggling.
A free being could only praise what could not be described.
Every bit of the known relaxed in this wonderment of peace.
Hallelujah!

March 11, 2012

Eyes Covered

My eyes covered with leaves, jewels, dirt
Falling back, quietly untangling my life's stories
Fears, longings...
Who is that child?
Underneath quiet eyes that sparkle,
Who knows me so well?

Exploring Faith

In a world of shifting sands
One sees the hawk
Perched in our valley,
Calm, devoted to all movement
In the green sparkling grasses.
The crow dive-bombs him,
"This is my roof, my territory, my meditation hall,
My stories, my thoughts.
How dare you intrude?"

Stand on this edge,
The merciless, sweet sound of your own voice,
Never convincing you to jump.
The taste of salt and dry mouth
And the blood from your own bitten lip.

Who told you, you could out-think this life,
Weighing all things with your golden intelligence,
That jumping into complete silence,
The sheer darkness,
Wouldn't have consequences,
No matter how courageously you struggled?

Yet, your own redemption,
This simple gesture,
A Buddha touching the earth,

Dissolving the madness of centuries,
A hawk poised on the edge of roof
About to drop off into
Darkness of the unknown.

Only two possibilities:
Find something solid to stand on
Or
You will be taught how to fly.

Faith comes in confirmation,
Like electricity unseen,
Yet it lights your path.

Retreat at Spirit Rock Meditation Center; March 10, 2011

Even-Mindedness (Full Moon)

Returning from so many journeys,
Stories piled on top of stories,
Closing chapter after chapter.
In some small cave, hidden away
Some text,

Forgotten for centuries,
Held tightly in the silence,
This river of our own mythology.

You, who have abandoned yourself
One too many times,
Have finally sat down.
Knowing nothing is forgotten in this place—
Only amplified,
This meditation hall filled to the brim.

Step back and move out of this house of dreams,
Into your own center,
Holding this lacquered begging bowl,
Holding last year's dreams over it,
Knowing this simple gesture.
Hands open,
Dropping it leaf by leaf,
Into this bottomless bowl.

I was here to celebrate
After all this living, bargaining over,
A place where the hummingbirds come
To taste the sweetness of your own openness.
The insecurity slips at last,
The rain washes it down
The green hillside
Into the creek, undistinguished
From tears or just the toxins of growing up.

Sitting, like a stone Buddha,
Unmoved by the longings and dislikes.
Now, no need to move away from the Great Suffering
Or even be enchanted by the Great Joy.
One sits in even-mindedness, with a boundless heart.
Earth, water, fire, air
Find no footing here.

One rests, the exile is over.
To praise form and the formless
A world where Emptiness, just the word,
Brings your hands together,
Gives way to a bow
In the great understanding.

You know now when they use the words
Luminous or boundless
It is no stranger.
You know you can sit in the Unknowing.
Blessed by a taste of grace.

Retreat at Spirit Rock Meditation Center; March 19, 2011

The Sweat Lodge

Enveloped in darkness.
Sitting up,
Fetal position,
Bodies touch in the circle lodge,
Pores opening,
Sage drifting in the steam,
Voices without faces or names,
Others' prayers mixing in my thoughts,
Feeling their pain, my pain; their hope, my hope,
Drifting with drum,
Eagle whistle,
Song,
Pulling the poisons out of our bodies, speech, and mind,
Allowing "separateness" to mingle,
Until earth, sky, water, fire are what they are
Leaving only gratitude.

July 17, 2005

The World Calling
(from a well gone dry)

From this silence so well constructed
I wander off into tomorrow—
bending like a willow
trying to touch a world unhatched,
this impossible of my imagination.
I am the intimacy of faith;
I am the grandeur of loneliness;
I am the worthiness
that which is kept buried beneath the wounds of my
stories.

Sometimes everything has to be studied.
Knowing, somehow, this sitting here is not enough.
This knowing, the fierce walking
—Like pilgrims through the darkness—
Knowing we've traveled inside everyone.

Feeling the grief, the joys
I want to know
No more traveling on the wings of fear and hope,
But sit by the fire of living,
No longer dying to what could have been
Or even what will be.

But finding my place in the things that are
Some mystery presented
Some grace
Some bit of mercy
Miraculously lived

So let this listening
Somewhere beneath the granite shelves of the earth
Where the sweet waters lie in wait
Be tapped to give life back to itself.

This basic goodness
This first step home
Gives you back to yourself
The heart flowing with each encounter
A mind pliable, moving like the sweet stream
From that deep down listening.

I am awake.
The world calls in its pungent need to change me,
I move into it, with it.

First Talk after Illness; August 17, 2009

Frog Clarity

Was it the concert given by the frogs
or the Dharma talk that was louder
than the chatter of my own mind
Until the wild roar stopped?

A silence descended through the hall,
Stillness untroubled by breath of that forgotten place.
Your own voice refused to move your delinquent thought words,
Adjusted, without movement, the quiet fury of the stillness—almost forgotten.

Like the great hunter you tracked that breath,
enlivened and focused.
Respectfully balanced a bedazzled heart and this well-crafted discernment.
You who came to this place longing for child's eyes that had grown accustomed to loss,
This river of aliveness floated on the mind's inward attention.

Frogs came alive again but this time breathing life.
Some great stillness untouched by the sounds,
Breath, body, mind-heart placed on the pinpoint in time,
Everything lined up for a fraction of a moment.

Your mind knowing this emptiness
Heart knowing this fullness
All bargaining over
You have arrived.

September 16, 2012

Full Moon Metta Talks

Oh, you thought I could talk about the heart:
The subtle way the armor shifts,
The many layers that hold it in place
And cover it with trance,
Or the ice that chills the fear
And freezes the heart.

At night, even the light through the window shades
Asks the moon to come
And press its face against mine,
Yes, breathes into me,
Closing the dream world;
Eyes open, 3 a.m.,
Shutting off the world of words.
A soundless shadow of the heart
Knowing, like a bird nesting,
Would gather all our flaws in celebration.

Could it be uncovering another layer?
Breath, wedded to both body and mind,
Seemingly uncomplicated and unfabricated,
This small movement,
The smallest shifts,
Allows heart, freed from its trance,
To shine like the moon,
Undiluted by the window shades of our stories.

To merge with it perfectly, impossibly,
It opens and closes,
"The sure heart's release,"
A promise given by the awakened one
Thousands of years ago.

I know, you know, we know.
I remember, you remember, we remember.
That's enough, you're enough, this is enough.
The eye drops off to sleep.

March 2, 2009

Moon Lost

Clouds covering the smallest
Wedge of light.
Standing in the puddles looking
For the moon.
Gone from this world.

Nowhere to be found—looking up
And down, in front, behind,
To each side. Lost!

Seeking it, longing for it,
Bending in every direction,
Falling to my knees.

Moon comes up to greet me.

December 28 2004

Cognizant Heart

The mirror unstained
Reflecting a spring day,
Frogs entering with great songs,
Thoughts thinking.
Crows cawing.
Old wounds calling.

Wonder of wonders.

Ah! But the lunch line remembers.
The septic pump soaks up the darkness.
Remember to invite that part that limps,
Staggering under the weight,
Determined to allow the movie star
Embrace the cripple.
Bringing the luminous mind to bear
To witness the fire of the heart.

March 8, 2005

Journeying

Color bursts onto retina.
Grass and trees wash clean.
Entrance eyes, ears, nose, mind...
A California spring bursts toward summer.
This valley vibrates towards its own creation.

Silence, keenly decreed,
Only wind blows,
Can actually speak in this inhabited valley.
Speaks only the language of leaves and branches
rubbing.

We came to this enchanted valley
So human silence
Could tear bitterly at the closed places.
You know: the betrayals, pains, regrets...
Moments of all sorts—lost forever,
Good and bad—drowned in all of time.

Slowly, to regain fundamental clarity,
Afternoon winds blow new thoughts down,
Down to the great highway.
Remembering—holding to anything—is not the point.

Could it be like waking from a dream.
A clear buoyant mind,

Wide like the sky,
Has no need of an object?

Finds some balance,
These factors awaken themselves,
This crucible of a teeter-totter
Balances on the head of a pin.
Everything comes to this center point.
The known world vanishes.
Mind in its dualism
Has lost its home.

All separateness
Untrue.

May 22, 2011

Life Happening Too Fast

Clouds covering the open sky
—blueness gone, gray holding the heavens—
this first day, wobbling is like this.
Shades of sleepiness,
mind spinning,
holding court with memories,
body resisting—creaking or was it just hollering,
"Why did I come?"

Some small gesture,
sit up straight.
Remember the sadness
—no one can be saved—
time takes a toll.
Heart sinks with truth.

How to begin again
knowing about endings?
Could it be so simple,
Letting go of everything?
Starting to practice again; breath appears
where no breath was noticed before.
Life is holding itself.

These magical displays:
Breath enters—a subtle relationship—

Giving and taking,
A wilderness of unforeseen chaos
reorganizing itself,
Inhale—exhale; in—out.

Could there be a place to rest
in this ferocity of change
—Elements dancing—earth, air, fire, water?
Oh yes, this knowing
has its place to rest readily available.
Mind dances in body.

Looking carefully— close in—
body and mind befriended—
a sense of ease.
I knew you came to awaken,
relaxing in the center of this pleasant, unpleasant dance.

Oh my! Bell rings
leaving the whole valley waiting.
All disappearing—reappearing
disappearing—reappearing.
Heart quivers.

May 16, 2011

Longing for Stillness

The clouds move through our Valley.
Drizzle, then perfect sunshine,
balancing the elements.
The sky too big for our own smallness.

Coming to this place with simple instructions,
The vulnerability of human intimacy is challenged
—Breathing into our own darkness—
being alone in our own arrogant selfishness.

Sitting allows the chaos of our world to gently yield:
Reaching out through the years,
Finding some grace—some medicine—
that shakes the heart and loosens our grasp.

Stepping out of a life so long ignored,
dipping back into one's uncertainty,
forgetting the strength of our own bones,
magnifying the prayer of this mysterious groundlessness,
softening, for some final blow

Having beaten the judger in ourselves thousands of
times;
Only to crack the old "selfishness",

What seemed like a battle becomes a symphony
holding a simple, wild, unfettered heart.
Our world open to the great stillness.

May 15, 2012

Mind-Fullness

Where was I
dancing on some distant past,
hoping, believing, this reminiscing could ultimately
change the past and empower the future magically?

Oh no, there I am messing with my life again
giving myself a headache
believing in this ultimate solution.
What kind of balderdash is this?

Knowing somehow this is not the practice,
tiger chasing its tail,
going in mental circles endlessly,
trying to outthink my own thinking.

How much simpler could it be,
letting go of one's thought constructions,
mind-full of this holy presence,
weaving forgetfulness with this remembering.

Suddenly the little baby turkey chicks,
weave themselves through the windy tall grass,
illuminating the joy of the one who is fully present,
having known what to do all along.
Yielding everything to the present.

May 12, 2015

Waking Up to the Dark

Oh yes, we came to rest in that silence,
Knowing somehow that our curious past,
With all its ferocity, was dragging us down
Onto this restless seat.

Oh, these teachings of respecting
The power of the night and its long darkness,
That infinite contraction when fear
Grasps our sanity and throws us down
The stairwell into the basement of our minds.

How could this be about liberation?
Struggling with the inevitability of change
And an aging body,
Yet, there are these moments...

Small little cracks,
Where life begins to know itself.
We are more than our stories,
Or even our struggles.

When the stillness of the dark is at its zenith,
And the light has slipped under the carpet,

Giving us another chance, redemption close at hand,
Questioning identity and these inherited,
Constructed views.

Having done some of the work to turn ourselves inside-
out,
Turning the mind/heart on itself
    —lo and behold—
That primordial, natural, pure awareness,
Which has been with us ever since birth
    —unblemished—
Was our home all along.

Saints, Sinners, Sages

Daringly dashing against the world of this and that,
Completely consumed by a raging fire,
Drowning under a torrent of people's desire to escape
From the presence of "just here".
Giving themselves to concepts,
Believing "to know" is to be of one mind.
And they waddle around discussing why that was then,
Thinking, thinking, clinging madly to the hope
That it will suddenly happen forever,
"Lightning in a clear blue sky".

The mind unstained in essence needs nothing
And the babbling brook is what it is.
Naropa, a matrix of this and that, vomits its guts daily.
Names of a thousand Klapas, rise and fall:
> Ram Dass, Bhagavan Das, Ani Tsultrim, Thubten Yeshe,
> Swami Muktananda, Allen Ginsberg, Pir Vilayat Khan,
> Father Doyle, Jack Kornfield, Joseph Goldstein, Robert Hall,
> Trungpa Rinpoche.
Clowns, performers, poets, saints and sages—
Enmeshed in a modular of gathering together. "Hum."

The diamond scepter reflects its nature on a crystal
bottle of sake,

Staggers and confuses the rascal mind leaving little or
nothing to work with.

Holy of holies

Pon (Long Gone John) Dharma, nomad-alias John
Travis; Naropa; July 1974

John Travis, Terri Clifford, and Lama Tsultrim Allione

Sitting Up Straight

Sitting up straight,
Correcting ourselves over and over,
Dedicating ourselves to the good,
Beyond ambition, beyond attainment,
Yet some deep down longing.
Correcting posture over and over.

Knowingly developing this fearless openness,
Reestablishing, maintaining flexibility and resilience,
Knowing no place better to cultivate this sanity,
Determined to stay in the center of our pillow.

The posture can be lost so easily.
Darkness creeps under my wandering thoughts
Coveting the smallest little sparkles,
Dragging me 100 miles from here.

How to avoid these seductive cries?
Stories seem more real than this place I sit.
How to overcome the sharp edge of a dead past
Or conjure up a perfect future?

Sometimes simplicity and strength,
Come into the sheer foundation of your own loveliness,
Living so close to this gut feeling of peace and ease.

The fire of your own voice sings praise to all awakening.

Curled up in front of the fire at home at last,
Knowingly bowing to the darkness,
Old friend coming in the back door,
Ushering itself out the front door.

Straightening up again mind at rest in soft heart.

December 12, 2012

The Great Rain

The grand oaks, blades of grass, soil shriveled and empty of moisture,
Waiting patiently without emotion, a day when the sky opened.
Teardrops from the heavens quenching the earth's thirst.
Everything opening so it can fully be its aliveness.

One moment longing, another moment filled to the brim.
Soil, trees, beyond enough so it races downhill,
Pulling all loose things down towards the mouth of the universal ocean,
Low spots filled, the veins of the earth rushing down toward its own merging.

A good day to see that nothing holds on, not for the minutest of time.
Awake, to every sense door, finding no home in them,
Heart sinks, as all contaminated states shake us.
Our core finds no rest in this transient world flowing by.

This attempt at finding ground, a solid me to hang my hat on,

Was this just a trick finding this inflated or maybe deflated mirage?

Again, floating downstream, no winning or losing here,

Just a heart bent towards ease; freedom close at hand.

Full Moon/March Retreat; March 1, 2012

The Secret: Ordinariness

Walking out into the center of the field,
Standing in the center of myself,
Mind looking at mind,
Watching the sun set,
The new moon rises.
Over and over this cycle repeats itself.

Standing in the center of the field,
The thousand faces carved in memory,
Stories remembered, so well crafted
Covering the heart like the clouds hiding the moon.

The bonfire spent, leaving unburnt,
Pieces of the heart scattered everywhere.
Bones from the old fires gather like firewood
Having collected them all,
Laying them on an altar of silk,
Worshipping them hoping they don't rot and decay like
our dreams.

Squeezing every bit of time out of them,
Hoping they will light again,
Giving back the bonfire of the heart.

Noting the leaning forward,
We make the subtle shift again, "a Buddha"
Sitting on his zafu.

Retreat at Spirit Rock Meditation Center; March 20, 2007

Ready or Not

Sitting on the bench,
meditation hall held in fog,
the path winding down,
down past the dining hall
stretching out towards the world.

Sitting in remedial fear
of the world,
kicked out of solitude
by the madness of my own life.

How can the sensitivity be translated?
How do these sweaty palms find a home?

Breathing,
    touching my own hand,
knowing somewhere deep down
touch is always available.

Not out there, in here.
Stepping out into a world
so consumed by itself

Standing,
    feeling body,
        small shiver
as the becoming and the fear rise together.

Can you ever be ready?
Stepping back into the life
you have so carefully crafted
out of all the old wounds and successes.

Is it possible to stand in the center
unmoved by the tides of change,
awake, collected,
heart listening to all the subtle clues?

Why not today?
Awake, at ease, remembering,
remembering the monastery bell.
How it rang...
    yet left
        no trace.

Ready?
Yes, ready

January 2, 2009

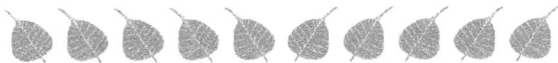

SEASONS

New Year

Walking out into the courtyard
With all my gremlins in tow,
Looking up into the sky,
Feet firmly planted, shouting "Here."
Sky vanishing, ground melting,
All reappearing.

2003

From the Silence (Winter Solstice)

Before freedom speaks
you must know,
know you lost something,
someone, somewhere, somehow.

When a small shiver—a vibration—
some tingling that causes your fingertips to stretch out
—out beyond time—
someplace where that budding awareness
leaves the foul taste and smell behind.

94

So a lucid calmness
like stepping through the clouds
being held in all directions,
your own strong arms
embraces that seer, that seeker,
the one who promised freedom,
your own body covered in rags,
a patchwork of so many dreams
caught in the destiny of becoming

Today you looked under the covers
far beneath the alluring senses
somewhere where a warm heart and fierce eyes and feet
free to walk
among the high mountains again,
unmoved but the chill of last year's dying.

Needing only a moment of full attention
the whole world disappears,
all the grasping to belong... gone,
all the constructions useless.
This body-mind, interconditionality known,
wisdom—well-earned—sees the natural state of things.
Oops! The heart breaks open.

December 22, 2010

Will We Ever Wake Up (Solstice)

When will we ever wake up?
Destined to sit in our own
Darkness,
Clamoring for our own redemption.

Such an apocalyptic culture
Caught in the vortex of absolute endings.
Innocence gifted back to us only when
We've given ourselves over to our fears-anxieties.

Clouds down around our ankles.
Damp and gray wrapped in our own bodies and raingear.
The long calendar of the Mayans
Destined to start another
Solar cycle.
Hooray, another chance.

Sitting still, somehow trusting the current,
Open to an unmoored boat floating downstream
Deadlines, schedules, appointments,
A world with constant demand.

Breaks my heart, over and over.
The faces of small children lost to a future,

Seeing the open innocence of my three grandchildren,
Wondering what pain those Connecticut families must
feel.

This sitting here, heroically,
Loving the small voice underneath.
Deep below the obvious.
Some sanity reconnected, wisdom found.

Dissecting the personal over and over, to nausea.
Slowly stepping back, separating content from the
Vast space. Relaxing in all the small spaces.
The sky has no limits.

Somehow knowing the heart understands.
All separateness was untrue.
Welcoming us to the new paradigm.
Wisdom with compassion flying off into the future.
The joy can be catching.
Blessings!

December 21, 2012

Sitting on the Bench (Spring Equinox)

Sitting on a bench...

A brazen turkey with the club foot
knows the human predator is
suspended in these wandering yogis.
Knows, somehow, they are taken by something greater,
knows their first utterances
—overheard only by themselves—
drops them deeper
into the silence of this impossible place.

A white tailed kite, sits so still,
suspended above our valley
—both wings in unison—
hovering at the edge of its own
insubstantialness,
body still, eyes everywhere.

Here the visible and invisible
show us how our ego
—mad mind—
dreams on and on.
Questioning what's real, who's real,
heralding the ancient panic.

Here on this ground, the wave breaks
leaving you only sky,
—vast empty sky—
a groundlessness
that sparks the panic,
which lights the flame again.

One wing holds us above the valley
empty
—maybe just emptiness—
In the other, some old flame with its warmth
and uncompromising light.
One holds the void; the other touches our world.

You knew you came to die.
Seeing through all the fabricated selves
the warmth and light are the only things left.

Please take my hand!
The world knows you.
They have been waiting
—sanity and compassion—
Yesterday this was me; today... not sure

Retreat at Spirit Rock Meditation Center; March 21, 2009

Before Freedom (Spring Equinox)

The gurgling of the creek
asks only one thing,
"Can you move with me?"
Teaching is never the same twice
—just moving—
asking to trust the impossible of waiting.

How to breathe this aloneness
poised on a ledge of spring?
Everything waiting
—bees, flies, you, me—
trembling from the earth's power of renewal.

You came to this place
knowing only faith could carry you across the threshold.
Some fierce love
—so deeply buried—
Some moments
—so long forgotten—
rise out of the clear mind-heart,
that keenly feels its lightness, brightness
wants to be found, to come alive
to its own delight and joy and steadiness

and let the darkness recede.

This great posture
—unmoved by small discomforts—
sitting, an ancient Buddha
reveals an upward spiral moving toward a moment
—a moment of disappearing—
following up all the way up to nowhere,
step-by-step.

Moving back into the known
—this becoming—
grabs the smallest sound in time.
Bang!
Your sensitivity yells, "Ouch!"
Caught, trapped, struggle,
had enough of this dying?
"Please, please let go."

No wish, no need, only to journey down with gravity,
revelations occur,
"We were never not whole."
Blessed and blessed again
by the emptiness, the nakedness of it all.
We have to give up everything to sit here,
the eyes of a wise-one and the heart of a child.

Retreat at Spirit Rock Meditation; March 1, 2010

Photograph of John Courtesy of Steve Solinsky (2020)

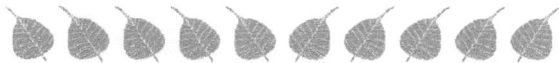

About the Author

John M. Travis is the founder of Mountain Stream Meditation Center and remains its guiding teacher. His teachings have been important to the growth and development of Buddhism and meditation throughout Northern California and several other areas in the Western United States.

John began his spiritual journey in Asia in the 1960s, a journey that continues today. He recalls:

I hitchhiked from London across Europe to India. Something was pulling me, but I didn't know what. I traveled overland and got busted in Thessalonika, Greece. They thought I was spy, because I had long hair and a peace sign on my backpack. I was placed in a straight-backed chair with bright lights on my face and grilled by guys in trench coats and hats. It was a scene right out of some grade-B movie. Finally, I made it to

Eastern Turkey, where I was thrown in jail again. It was just one crazy thing after another, but I knew where I was headed.

That fall, I was in Nepal when locals were having a black-hat ceremony for His Holiness the Sixteenth Karmapa. I looked at his picture and recognized him as a face I had seen in Boulder Creek, California, during a fevered bout of hepatitis a year earlier. My friends and I attended the ceremony. When I walked into the room where the Karmapa sat, he immediately said to me, "Oh, I know you." He became my first and primary teacher for Tibetan Buddhism.

John sat with Buddhist masters in India, Tibet, Nepal, Myanmar, Thailand, and other Eastern regions. While in Asia, he traveled with Ram Dass, through whom he connected with Maharaj-ji Neem Karoli. He also studied with Lama Thubten Yeshe and the Venerable Kalu Rinpoche. John later entered the ashram where he took full Hindu monastic ordination under the guidance of Swami Satyananda Saraswati.

John travels extensively both in the United States and around the world. He leads retreats throughout the United States and pilgrimages to sacred Buddhist sites in India and Nepal. Recently he and a group visited sacred Mount Kailash in Tibet.

In 1970 John began his studies in the Vipassana tradition with Anagarika Munindra and later became a student of S.N. Goenka and took full monastic ordination in 1979 under the Venerable Taungpulu Sayadaw. John devoted himself to Senior Teacher Training with Jack Kornfield at Spirit Rock Meditation Center from 1989 to 1993. Upon graduation he was ordained in the Vipassana tradition of Mahasi Sayadaw and Ajahn Chah and authorized to teach in that tradition. Today he is senior teacher emeritus at Spirit Rock.

In 1986, John began teaching weekly meditation groups in Nevada City, California. This eventually evolved into today's meditation center. During weekly Dharma talks, John incorporates teachings and insights he gained from his extensive travels and his personal spiritual practice.

In 2019 John published his first book, *Taking the One Seat*, based on his Dharma talks given during classes and retreats.

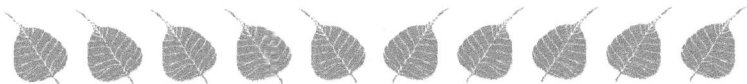

Editor's Notes

John is a poet and his poetry is very personal to him. He expresses himself more profoundly in these poems than he can in a Dharma talk. Over the years he has been protective of his poetry and reluctant to approve publication. I am deeply honored that he entrusted me with publishing his most personal thoughts and expressions. Reading and rereading these poems provided me with a deeper insight into John, the Buddha's teachings and the path to relieve suffering.

John asked that we limit the number of poems to sixty-four, a spiritual and meaningful number in Chinese culture. I have divided them into three sections:

- The first, "The Trek", focuses on his multiple trips to Asia and the teachings of the masters in whose presence he sat and studied;
- The second, "The Cushion", includes poems he composed to share with his retreatants or for Dharma talks;
- And the third section, "The Seasons", focuses on the solstice and the equinox.

These poems incorporate many insights from his Asian travels and experiences so there is often no clear delineation between "The Trek" and "The Cushion". I accept full responsibility for the decision for choosing to place a particular poem in one section or the other.

I am grateful for Spirit Rock Meditation Center and for Mountain Stream Meditation Center for preserving much of John's poetry and making it available to me. Without the diligence of these two centers, this work would not have been possible.

I am also indebted to my wife Lori, who also read and reread this manuscript with a keen eye that picked up subtleties that I had missed. In addition, she provided encouragement and support throughout this project.

Mostly, I am deeply moved that John allowed me to share these personal insights that came through him. I have greatly benefited from editing this book of John's poetry. I hope his work will touch you as it has touched me. Thank you, John, for the privilege and honor of editing these gems.

Coy F. Cross II, Editor

Image Notes

Photographs were taken inside the Mountain Stream Meditation / Nevada City Insight Center (2019)

Photographs were taken on the grounds of the Mountain Stream Meditation / Nevada City Insight Center (2019); Courtesy of Steve Solinsky

Photograph of John (left), Terri Clifford (center), Lama Tsultrim Allione (right).
Terri Clifford studied Tibetan medicine in Tibet. While there she contacted a form of encephalitis.
Lama Tsultrim Allione founded and still runs Tara Mandala, the International Buddhist Community at Pagosa Springs, Colorado.

Photograph of John Courtesy of Steve Solinsky

Photographs of John were taken on the grounds of the Mountain Stream Meditation Nevada City Insight Center (2020); Courtesy of Steve Solinsky

Photograph of the Dharma Wheel of Life at the Sun Temple Konark, Orissa, India taken by Ramnath Bhat. It was modified from Wikimedia Commons (the free media repository). This file is licensed under the Creative Commons Attribution 2.0 Generic license (https://commons.wikimedia.org /wiki/File: %272%27_Dharma_Wheel_ the_Wheel_of_Life_ at_Sun_Temple_Konark,_Orissa_India_February_2014.jpg)

"Mud Footsteps" Courtesy of Dayna Hubenthal

Engage with John M. Travis

John Travis on Facebook
https://www.facebook.com/john.travis.1069020

John Travis on the Web - For more information about John Travis's pioneering spiritual work or for audio and video files of John's teachings in the Mountain Stream Meditation archives visit Mountain Stream Meditation's website: https://www.mtstream.org/our-teachers/

John Travis At Mountain Stream Medication Center – John is the guiding and founding teacher of the center. Everyone is welcome there and we offer a broad range of programs, classes and one day retreats to meet our community's interests and practice needs. We also host residential retreats at various venues two to three times per year. Our center is located at 710 Zion Street, Nevada City, California 95959.

Other books by John M. Travis – In his debut book, *Taking the One Seat* (forward by Jack Kornfield), John teaches Buddha's insights in order to relieve suffering in daily life. The book is based on a number of John's Dharma talks.

"John Travis brings 50 years of contemplative practice alive in the words of this book. He has explored the Dharma in many forms: as a wandering holy sadhu in India, a dauntless yogi and courageous spiritual adventurer, as a poet and a meditator, as a student of a hundred spiritual teachers, and as a beloved teacher himself, a father and husband and community builder and all along, a lover of the Path of the Heart." - Jack Kornfield

Use the QR codes below to buy the book, *Taking the One Seat*, at Barnes & Nobles or other online stores.

Buy now: Barnes & Noble

Buy now: Amazon

Spirit Rock Meditation Center

Spirit Rock Meditation Center is set among 411 acres of serene oak woodlands in West Marin County, California. It's a refuge and a place to transform by living more wisely and kindly. What sets us apart is spaciousness, stillness, caring teachers, staff and volunteers. We create a supportive environment for turning inward and letting go of the struggles that interfere with the experience of freedom and joy inherent in every moment.

Dharma, Vipassana, and Metta are at the heart of all the programs offered at Spirit Rock through a breadth of formats to fit anyone's schedule, needs and meditation experience—from two-hour, drop-in classes and daylong events to silent residential retreats lasting three-days to two months. We offer advanced practitioner programs (a year or more) and online classes. To find out more about Spirit Rock Meditation Center and to contact us, come to our website at https://www.spiritrock.org.

John Travis earned Teacher Emeritus at Spirit Rock.

www.ingramcontent.com/pod-product-compliance
Lightning Source LLC
Chambersburg PA
CBHW020441100426
42812CB00036B/3406/J